HAIR STORIES

40 Wisdom-Filled Devotionals

Joanna McGee Bradford

Hair Stories. 40 Wisdom-Filled Devotionals

MacKenzie Publishing
Halifax, Nova Scotia
ISBN - 978-1-927529-75-1
January 2020

Editor: C.A. MacKenzie

MacKenzie Publishing

Dedication

To women, with or without hair…
To know and love yourself
is to express beauty in the world.
Be your own kind of beautiful.

Joanna

Contents

Foreword

H*air Stories* is a thoughtful collection of stories by women for women. Women often view their hair as an integral part of the WHOLE self. Hair is, in fact, a part of the whole person.

Joanna McGee Bradford has afforded women an opportunity to share their hair stories through memorable moments and light laughter. She has a focused ability to link hair stories to various situations that offer life lessons for the reader regardless of race or ethnicity.

News headlines and reports continue to emerge about hair, identity, and discrimination. Enter the CROWN Act (Creating a Respectful and Open World for Natural Hair). This Act is yet one more indirect reminder that the identity of blacks, and particularly the natural hair they are born with, is still being questioned. The CROWN Act was put in place to address and eliminate the discrimination. The elimination of discrimination may then promote inclusiveness.

In 2020, how dare anyone question a woman about the state of her hair. Hair is a part of the innate self. In a global society where equity and inclusion are often mentioned in the conversation, all hair types and styles should be valued and appreciated. Thus, we ought to value the identity of each individual, including the hair on one's head. You love your hair, and the process of loving yourself begins.

Dr. Sharon Sanders-Funnye

Introduction

Friends always commented on my ever-changing hairstyles. In some ways, my hair reflected the struggles I had with embracing my authentic self. I liked my hair's texture but gave in to the voices that said straight hair would be more acceptable. I struggled between trying to fit in but wanting to wear styles I admired and felt drawn to adopt for myself. It took many years—and more hairstyles—before I became content with who I was while understanding that change was part of the process. Once I accepted myself, I was able to embrace whatever style, head-covering, or other hair adornment I chose.

Despite the battles I'd had with hair, my passion for writing remained constant. I'd see, hear, or experience something and jot it down to include in a book. I'd marvel at the simplest things and think of how it related to God. Those musings became devotionals. With my many hairstyles and experiences, I had enough to fill a book. However, as others shared their stories with me, I realized their voices also deserved to be heard.

Hair Stories contains the wit and wisdom of women just like you. These stories will help you in celebrating the journey to become your best self, regardless of your hair texture or style. As you meditate on these devotionals, let God's word empower you to embrace and love every part of you, a woman of confident grace, secure in who she is and who she is becoming.

Joanna McGee Bradford

DELIGHTING IN YOUR IDENTITY

"Loving oneself isn't hard, when you understand who and what 'yourself' is. It has nothing to do with the shape of your face, the size of your eyes, the length of your hair or the quality of your clothes. It's so beyond all of those things and it's what gives life to everything about you. Your own self is such a treasure."

—Phylicia Rashad

Wonderfully Made

"I need to see my own beauty and continue to be reminded that I am enough... that I am beautiful... that the texture of my hair ... are all worthy and okay."
—Tracee Ellis Ross

I hardly recognized Barb. The woman standing across from me, engaged in an animated conversation, had a nape-length, wavy bob styled in a loose and free playful fashion. When we'd met a few months earlier, her hair had been blow-dried and curled. To keep everything in place, she had sprayed her hair until stiff strands covered her features. Now, she looked much livelier, even younger.

I walked over to Barb. "I love your hair. Did you get it cut?"

She grinned. "No. I was styling it wrong." Barb explained she'd gone to lunch with a former classmate, whose thick wavy brown hair was like hers.

"She told me about using mousse for my hair type, scrunching it up, and just letting it be. I was always trying to tame my hair. Now that I understand how to care for it, I don't fight with my hair. It takes half the time of using a blow dryer and curling iron." She shrugged. "I used to think I just had 'bad' hair."

Barb discovered the valuable secret in bringing out her best was respecting the way she had been designed. God says that his creations are good.

When he created the world, for five days he *spoke* things into existence. "Let there be light … Let there be a space between the waters …" When it came to human beings, scripture says he *created* them, male and female in his image (Genesis 1:26). What was God's response to his creation? "God saw all that he had made, and it was very good" (Genesis 1:31, NIV).

God wasn't having an off day when he thought of the one-of-a-kind design known as YOU. He saw you before forming you in the womb that became your first cradle. You are wonderfully made (Psalm 139:13-16). When you were born, God didn't snap his fingers. "Ooops! I messed that one up." From the bottom of your feet to the crown of your head—regardless of the hair covering it—God considers it and you as "good."

Look in the Mirror

Study yourself in the mirror. Don't just take a glance and turn away. Note your hair. What do you notice? What do you like? What about your facial characteristics or body type? Do you have high cheekbones? Expressive eyes? Try to identify at least three things you like about yourself. How can you enhance those attributes even further? If there's something that vexes you about your appearance, pray to value those things while also learning how to bring out its beauty.

Prayer

Lord, you made me the way I am. Even before placing me in my mother's womb, you knew me and said I was "good." Your design is not flawed. You are a master craftsman and I am your masterpiece. Amen.

Beautiful

"The beauty of a woman is not in the clothes she wears, the figure that she carries or the way she combs her hair."
—Audrey Hepburn

Nyoka enjoys a variety of styling options, including wigs and extensions in every hue and length. One week, she sported three different looks. Day one: bouncy layers of black corkscrew curls. Mid-week: same look, but dark brown with caramel highlights. On Friday, short finger waves donned her head. Co-workers complimented her hair and she thanked them before quickly beginning work, wanting to ensure everything was completed timely and accurately. She could be heard offering assistance, an encouraging word, or a bowl of her fabulous chili that she brought for everyone's enjoyment. Nyoka knows that the inner beauty of being kind and helpful will last longer than the outward beauty of hair and fashion styles that come and go.

In the 1920s, finger waves were popular, worn by stars like Bette Davis and Josephine Baker. "BIG HAIR" like the beehive rose in the 1950s and 1960s. Huge Afros in the late 1970s gave way to the 1980s Jheri curl. "Back in the day," many people wobbled on platform shoes, now called wedge heels. At a 2019 movie premiere, actress/singer/songwriter Beyoncé resurrected and updated the finger wave with braids.

What has been done will be done again (Ecclesiastes 1:9). Outward appearances constantly change while inward beauty is always in style.

In 1st Peter 3:3-4, the apostle directed wives to not be concerned about the outward beauty that depends on fancy hairstyles, expensive jewelry, or beautiful clothes. Now, don't get it twisted! When Peter wrote those words, he was talking to women who had escaped the slavery of the Egyptians only to become a slave to beauty. There's a difference between a routine of self-care versus being ruled by a beauty routine. His message to wives is wise counsel for anyone.

Who doesn't appreciate the intricate ways that hair can be styled? It can be twisted, twirled, braided, adorned with jewelry, or lengthened. Beauty and style are fleeting. However, the beauty of a gentle and quiet spirit lasts forever.

Look in the Mirror

Do your eyes sparkle with more beauty than the jewels you wear? Is your lipstick more flattering to your mouth than the words coming out of it? Are you draped with a quiet, poised confidence and not relying upon man-made garments? Don't allow outer appearance to become your beauty standard. Let God develop your inner spirit to reflect his glory and leave a lasting impression.

Prayer

Heavenly Father, help me to remember that external appearances change. I pray that the beauty in my heart lives on in the lives I touch. Amen.

Chosen

"And I am going to tell you like this, 'If you can't love me with short hair, and you telling me I got to have long hair to be loved, guess what, I ain't the one for you.'"
—Jada Pickett Smith

Darlene carries the glow of a woman who is deeply loved by her husband. She didn't realize the depth of his feelings until she risked telling him about her hair.

A year before they married, her hair started breaking from relaxers. She began wearing a protective hairstyle to prevent further damage. The extensions cascaded down her back. Men yelled, "You sure look good!" She brushed off the compliments with a toss of her head—except when she caught Thomas's eye. They wed after a six-month courtship.

A year later, she wanted to straighten her natural hair and remove the extensions. However, she feared Thomas wouldn't like the change. She took the risk by removing them and braced for her husband's reaction.

"You're beautiful," Thomas said upon seeing her. "I love everything about you, including whatever way you choose to style your hair."

"How could I have doubted?" Darlene wondered. "I was chosen for him."

It can be scary to reveal yourself differently from the way you've always appeared. However, claiming your identity is worth the risk.

The Bible's Queen Esther faced that same dilemma when she needed to reveal her secret to King Xerxes. He had already banished her predecessor, Queen Vashti.

Xerxes was drunk when he commanded Vashti to show her beauty before a gathering of men. She refused because royal women were not generally exposed to the public and the king's request was humiliating. At an adviser's suggestion, Xerxes issued an order forbidding her from ever entering his presence (Esther 1:9-20). Four years later, Esther was crowned queen.

Xerxes didn't know Esther was Jewish. When he signed a decree to destroy the Jews, Esther's cousin requested she appeal to the king. She faced a double dilemma: revealing her nationality and risking her life by approaching the king without being summoned. She requested that the Jewish people join her and her attendants in fasting; then, she'd proceed even if she perished (Esther 4:16). Xerxes spared Esther's life and that of her people.

Just as Esther and Darlene were chosen by God, so were you. Scriptures remind us of this. "You didn't choose me. I chose you" (John 15:16, NLT). Never doubt God's love for you.

Look in the Mirror

Do you desire to make a change but are afraid of others' reactions? Identify what's holding you back. Being yourself includes everything about you. If you're confident in who God created you to be, others will be too.

Prayer

God, help me to see myself as you do. Help me come to the place where if I chose to be anybody, I would choose me as you've already done. Amen.

Set Apart

"My body is very different from most of the dancers I dance with. My hair is different than most I dance with. But I didn't let that stop me..."
—Misty Copeland

Yvette and I chatted over lunch at a popular B.B.Q. restaurant. Our conversation ranged from trying to locate the best ribs in town to finding the best way to style hair.

She cut into a slice of tender beef brisket. "My twelve-year-old niece scoops gobs of gel onto her hair and then brushes it with hard strokes, causing breakage. When I style her hair, so many flakes fall onto her shoulders. She wants to fit in with the girls at school who have long, straight hair. They think her hair is 'cool.'"

Both sets of girls—black and white—admired each other's hair. All hair has the same chemical composition, being mainly comprised of keratin. Emerging from the scalp, Caucasian and Asian hair follicles are round or oval. Black hair follicles are flat and tend to coil. The way in which hair is "expressed" from one's head accounts for its look and characteristics. Similar to how hair is metamorphosized from the head, God uses our differences in expression to attract others to him as he did with John the Baptist.

John was different than most religious leaders. Before he was born, his parents were told John would be set apart (Luke 1:15). He lived in the wilderness, wore clothes made of camel hair, and ate a strange diet of locusts and wild honey. His unorthodox appearance and bold teaching attracted crowds. Many people repented from their sins and asked to be baptized (Matthew 3:1-6).

You, too, have been set apart for a special purpose. It may be your speaking style. Perhaps it's how you grasp a spatial concept and turn it into an architectural drawing.

Your bold doodling isn't just graffiti, it's art. Verses such as Deuteronomy 14:2 provide assurance that God considers you as "...holy to the LORD your God, and he has chosen you from all the nations of the earth to be his own special treasure." God considers you a gem. A prize. Valuable.

Take heart in being different. Bishop T.D. Jakes said, "Don't be so busy trying to fit in that you lose your exclusivity." Savor the difference, the flavor to the world that only you bring.

Look in the Mirror

Most of us have experienced feeling different from others. You might be tempted to minimize or eliminate the differences. Rather than becoming part of a big melting pot, think of a salad bowl. Filled with ingredients having different textures, each retains its individuality so the results burst with flavor. The difference that sets you apart may be what God wants to use to win others to faith in Christ.

Prayer

Dear Jesus, thank you for being so creative in using different ways and people to tell your story. Help me to value my uniqueness and use it to share my faith. Amen.

Gifted

"We must believe that we are gifted for something, and that this thing, at whatever cost, must be attained."
—Marie Curie

My son, Marcus, ran a hand over his hair. "Mom, can you cut my Mohawk down?"

In keeping with high school tradition, varsity football players wore the distinctive hairstyle for the first few weeks of their senior year. Having shown off the style, and his status, Marcus was ready to return to his usual, less severe fade.

I hadn't cut a man's hair since butchering his dad's. Using a pick, I had lifted the springy strands before aiming the clippers. The hair recoiled after being sheared, leaving two deep indentations on either side of his head. Recalling the horror on his face, I told Marcus, "I'm not good at cutting hair."

"It'll be fine, Mom." He sat in a chair, wrapped a towel around his shoulders, and bent his head like a trusting, little lamb.

Unfortunately, the shears dipped a few times. "Oops!" I said, cutting too low in spots. Studying my handiwork, I grimaced before offering apologies to my son.

He smiled at me. "Don't worry about it, Mom. It'll be okay."

The next day, he returned home with a gray hoodie over his head. "I was able to handle the kidding for the first two periods. After that, I couldn't take it." He dropped his books on the kitchen counter before walking to his friend's house to have his head shaved.

Cutting hair is not my gift. Yet, God equips people with gifts and talents to serve others and honor him. We often think about gifts like evangelizing, leadership, and teaching. Indeed, the Evangelist Philip had four unmarried daughters who had the gift of prophecy (Acts 21:9). Certainly, Priscilla and Aquila were gifted teachers. When they heard the disciple Apollos speaking in the synagogue, they realized his knowledge was incomplete. The couple took him aside and taught him about Jesus' life, crucifixion and resurrection. Apollos became a better teacher. Even hairstyling and cutting can be a ministry.

When my friend and barber, Nate, cuts young men's hair, he talks with them about work, life, and Godly relationships. The apostle Paul compares spiritual gifts to the members of the body, each having an important function (1 Corinthians 12:12-18). Don't discount any interest, talent, or gift.

Can you sing? Do you enjoy working with children? Do you have a knack for making others at ease in your home? How do you put these talents to use? Gifts are often revealed as work or service is performed, not in being idle.

Look in the Mirror

Are there things you brush off as "no big deal" but cause others to marvel? Do you ever become so involved when "doing your thing" that you lose track of time or forget to eat? If you aren't sure of your gift, ask God to reveal it. Like a present, it is meant to be opened and enjoyed.

Prayer

Lord, you know how I've been wired. I want to honor you and love others with the gifts you've entrusted to me. Amen.

Overcomer

You cannot stop birds from flying over your head, but you can stop them nesting in your hair.
—African Proverb

Allison cringed when she remembered the day in second grade when a girl sitting behind her whispered, "What are those little beads on the back of your neck?"

"That's my hair," Allison said, hanging her head in shame about the tight, kinky hair along the nape of her neck. For the next fifty years, Allison thought of the question when relaxing her hair bone straight, shaving her neck clean, or wearing a wig long enough to cover the area.

Many people commented that Allison would look great with short hair. One day, a shopper in a beauty store eyed her. "You could wear a super-short cut with those cheekbones."

Allison smiled. "I've thought about it."

"What's stopping you?"

What are those little beads? How long had that question reverberated in her mind? *Why am I holding on to the words of a second-grader?* Allison decided to silence the voice. She made an appointment to have her relaxed hair cut short.

Two years later, she throws her head back and laughs. "Someone I wouldn't recognize today lived in my head for too long. I've got better things to think about."

The world's voices about our looks and identity shout long and loud. We must internalize what God says to overcome the noise, even when it's inside our heads.

When an angel of the Lord appeared to the farmer, Gideon, he called, "Mighty hero, the Lord is with you!" (Judges 6:11-14, NLT).

Gideon was hiding from marauding attackers. Picture him looking around, asking himself, *"Who, me?"* He tried explaining that his clan was the smallest and he was the least.

That didn't change God's mind about how he saw Gideon. Similarly, God is not going to be persuaded to change his opinions about you. From the beginning, God says we are created in his image (Genesis 1:27). He calls us his children (John 1:12). In Ephesians 2:10, we're told that we are his masterpiece. We are loved so much that Jesus Christ died for us (1 John 3:16). Like Allison, who triumphed over the lingering voice in her head, we are an overcomer (1 John 4:4).

We don't have to allow negative comments to nest in our thoughts. We are not our negative experiences. Allow God's views about you to shape your identity.

Look in the Mirror

In what ways have you been identified? The one not as smart as her sibling? The one who will never amount to anything? What words do you use to identify yourself? How does that line up with what God says? Memorize and recite aloud scriptures stating how God identifies you. Write affirmations. Place them where they can be easily seen.

Prayer

God, let me see through your eyes, for you see with your heart. Help me not to view myself as anything different than who you say I am. Amen.

Mindful

"If I want to knock a story off the front page,
I just change my hairstyle."
—Hillary Rodham Clinton

My first attempt at hair design would have gone viral—in a negative way. At thirteen, I no longer wore braids. I had transitioned to a press and curl. After sleeping overnight on foam rollers, I'd remove them and comb through the curls, finishing the ends with a little flip. Boring! I was ready for an updo.

Since my hair barely skimmed the base of my neck, I needed length. Now, imagine eighteen inches of flexible wire, covered with tufts of soft, curly synthetic hair. The hairpiece resembled a branch of an artificial evergreen Christmas tree, but with black leaves rather than green. I made a small bun with my hair, covered it with a toilet paper core and pinned it in place. I wound the hairpiece around it. With it soaring high on my head—like an antenna—I imagined being the envy of my classmates.

During school, the cardboard core loosened, weighed down by the weight of the hairpiece. I resembled a bobble-head doll by the end of the day. Holding my head stiffly and barely moving my neck, no one noticed before I quickly left the building. Had my fiasco happened today, it would've been broadcast and ridiculed on social media.

The early church didn't have Facebook, but news still traveled far. Two women, Euodia and Syntyche, got into a huge argument. Word of their feud reached the apostle Paul. He was almost 5,000 miles away—in prison. In his letter written to the Ephesian community, he pleaded with them to settle their disagreement (Philippians 4:2). He didn't want the dispute to interfere with telling others the good news of Jesus Christ.

Paul's words are relevant today. Before posting a message online, consider the psalmist's words, "May these words of my mouth and this meditation of my heart be pleasing in your sight, Lord" (Psalm 19:14).

The social media platform is powerful. We shouldn't use it to dish out discord or broadcast blunders. It is imperative that we be mindful of the message, and image, we project to the world.

Let it be a tool to demonstrate unity and the love of Jesus.

Look in the Mirror.

Consider your communications on social media. Looking for "likes"? Do your words show love? Demonstrate kindness? Illustrate integrity? Offer encouragement? Pause to consider whether your words reflect Christ.

Prayer

Dear Jesus, I pray to be mindful of what and how I say, whether it's spoken or written. I want my speech to reflect you. Amen.

Knowledgeable

"To watch how lovingly your children parent their own children is to know profound achievement."
—Sally Field

Avery hopped in the car after school and greeted her mom. "Remember that you promised to take my hair down before Grandma takes me to children's church."

As a busy, single mom of three, Denise had been delaying the task of removing her daughter's kinky twists. "Okay. We'll get it done." An idea popped into her mind once they got home. "I'll help you get started before I make dinner."

With Avery standing before the mirror, Denise lifted one of the twists. "Work from the bottom. Use your fingers to unravel each one." She tugged at the hair closest to the scalp where the extension was anchored. "This will be the hardest part since it holds the hair in place." She watched as Avery followed her example. "You're doing great! I'll come back to check on you."

When Denise returned twenty minutes later, Avery turned around and grinned, holding a pair of scissors. She had removed the extensions by cutting them out—along with chunks of her hair.

After dinner—and tears—Denise covered Avery's head with a scarf when her mother arrived to take the kids to children's church. While they were out, Denise glued hair to a stocking cap to make a wig for Avery. "I should've taken more time to teach Avery. But thank God Mom can help."

It's important to teach children skills such as maintaining a home, caring for their hair, and other basics to function in the world. Christian parents, grandparents, and other adults with spiritual influence must also anchor children in the truth of God's word for it has eternal implications.

Timothy received teaching in the Christian faith from his grandmother Lois and mother, Eunice. He became a part of the apostle Paul's missionary team and later became a minister. In his old age and final letter, Paul encouraged Timothy by reminding him of his roots, the faith which was demonstrated first in his grandmother and mother (2 Timothy 1:5).

Teaching a child about the things of God goes beyond everyday life. While making sure children are educated and able to function in the world, God instructs us to be responsible for their spiritual development. "Point your kids in the right direction—when they're old they won't be lost" (Proverbs 22:6, MSG). Nurturing a child's early faith has far-reaching implications, not just for them but for generations to come.

Look in the Mirror

Are you modeling character, grace, and mercy for your children and those who look up to you? Are you walking the talk? Does your child's behavior reflect the goodness and kindness you've demonstrated?

Prayer

Lord, teach me your ways. Show me how to teach my children and other young people so that they walk in the purpose for which they've been called. Amen.

Becoming Wise

"They're not gray hairs. They're wisdom highlights."
—Anonymous

Even wearing glasses and sitting close to the lamp, my mother was unable to guide the slender thread through the needle's eye. "Will you thread this for me?"

I wet the end with saliva and easily coaxed it through the tiny opening. "You can't see that?" I asked with amazement borne of youthful ignorance.

Mama gave a patient chuckle. "Just keep lying down and getting up. One day, you'll see."

Fast forward a few decades. I don't need glasses or lamp light to glimpse the silver strands woven through my hair. However, I need help threading a needle. Natural sight dims with age while Godly wisdom sharpens our perspective.

After Solomon became king, he asked for an understanding mind to rule the nation of Israel. God was pleased that Solomon didn't ask that his enemies be wiped out or for wealth. So, God gave him riches and honor as well as wisdom (1 Kings 3:7-13).

Some of Solomon's wisdom can be found in the book of Proverbs. It's filled with practical suggestions on living a Godly life. Consider the advice to be diligent in carrying out responsibilities. "Take a lesson from the ants, you lazybones. Learn from their ways and become wise!" (Proverbs 6:6, NLT).

To avoid conflict, Proverbs offers the guideline of, "Don't answer the foolish arguments of fools, or you will become as foolish as they are" (Proverbs 26:4). Also, there are wise thoughts and observations. "Gray hair is a crown of glory; it is gained by living a godly life" (Proverbs 16:31).

Youthfulness invariably gives way to age. Some things, such as physical strength and eyesight, diminish. Other things, like wisdom, grow with experience.

You might be fighting the gray hairs with hair color. Or, maybe you have chosen to embrace the silver vixen staring at you in the mirror. Wherever you are in the journey, consider the glorious crown of wisdom along with the gray hair on your head.

Look in the Mirror

Have you considered the "Proverbs 31 woman"? Fortunately, she is thought to be a *composite* of Godly women. (Whew! What a relief.) These wise habits can be used in the home, business, and relationships regardless of age. Identify the traits found in Proverbs 31 that you can incorporate into your life.

Prayer

Lord, as my years increase, may wisdom do likewise. I ask that it cover every fiber of my being. Amen.

Called

"My hair is only a part of who I am.
It does not define my whole self."
—Dr. Sharon Sanders-Funnye

Sharon was entering seventh grade when she developed ringworm on her scalp, leaving patchy areas of baldness. The cream prescribed by her doctor caused most of her remaining hair to fall out. She was left with sparse hair in front and a little at the crown. Her mother bought multiple scarves to hide the baldness.

Sharon learned artful ways to wrap scarves around her carefully guarded secret. Sometimes she left a few strands in front to cascade over her forehead. When she wanted to kick it up a notch, she swept the bangs to the side of her face.

Imagine the teasing from her classmates if they'd seen what was underneath the headwraps. *Baldheaded! Ringworm head!* Amazingly, Sharon didn't miss a single day of school for the entire time it took for her hair to grow back—almost two years. She loved school and had a passion for learning. Our passion is "tailor-made" to guide us toward our calling.

The prophet Elisha was called to deliver a message of repentance. The nation of Israel had turned away from God and had begun engaging in idolatry. As Elisha walked along the road, a mob of more than forty boys jeered at him. "Go away, baldy!" they chanted. "Go away, baldy!" Elisha turned around and looked at them, and he cursed them in the name of the Lord (2 Kings 2:23-25).

We don't have to curse those who would try to derail us from our purpose. We can nurture the passion God has placed in us.

At the college where Sharon now works, students have a name for her: "Dr. Funnye." She leads a program to ready students for post-secondary education. "All of my experiences have been connected, drawing me closer to my authentic self—my identity as an educator-leader and a passionate advocate for children."

God created us with a purpose. "He causes everything to work together for the good of those who love him and are called according to His purpose for them" (Romans 8:28, NLT). Not everything that happens to us is good. However, God will use it to fulfill his purpose.

Look in the Mirror

What excites you? Are you familiar with the expression, "Find something you enjoy doing and you'll never work a day in your life?" That's likely your passion. Are you working your passion or your hustle? Identify opportunities to step into your passion, even if it's just a few hours weekly. Even if there's no pay in dollars, God will reward you in his way.

Prayer

Dear God, please ignite my passion for the work you've called me to do. Help me get past negative experiences. I'm trusting your word that all things will work out for my good and your glory. Amen.

DEVELOPING DEEPER RELATIONSHIPS

*"If you can learn to love yourself and all the flaws,
you can love other people so much better.
And that makes you so happy."*
—Kristen Chenoweth

Helpful Friends

"True friends are those rare people who come to find you in dark places and lead you back to the light."
—Anonymous

"Are the parts in my hair even?" I bent my head and lifted my locks so my friend, Cynthia, could take a close look. I sighed, suspecting she'd confirm that I'd have to take my locks down. It's a time-consuming process, which anyone who has worn braids or locks, can testify to, understands, and dreads.

"Hmm," she said, lifting a section. "Give me your hand." She placed my finger on one of the thick coils. "Feel that? It's almost twice as big as the one next to it." She guided my hand, asking me questions until I accepted my fate.

"It'll take hours," I moaned.

Without hesitation, Cynthia said, "I'll help."

The next day, she plopped into my oversized red leather chair while I arranged myself on the floor. Our work took half the time than if I'd tackled the job alone. I was grateful that my friend had postponed tasks piling up at her own home to help me.

True friends find ways to help. This is what Jonathan did when his friend, David, was threatened by Jonathan's father, Saul. Twice, Saul hurled a spear at David. The friends concocted a plan for David to escape if Saul threatened David again.

One day, Saul flew into a rage and demanded that David be brought in so that he could kill him. Jonathan confronted his father and Saul threw his weapon at him (1 Samuel 18:10-20:33).

The next morning, the friends met, cried, and embraced. Jonathan said, "Go in peace, for we have made a pact in the Lord's name. We have entrusted each other and each other's children into the Lord's hands forever" (1 Samuel 20:42, NLT). Sometime after David became king, he brought Jonathan's son to live in the palace (II Samuel 10:13).

Most of us won't be in a situation where we promise to become the guardian of our friends' children. Nor is it likely we will have to risk our lives for someone else. However, we can help friends when they're "running on fumes." We can run errands. We can listen without interjecting opinions or rendering judgment. It might be offering our hands and time to assist with a project, preparing a meal—or picking one up. Scripture teaches that some friends are closer than family (Proverbs 18:24).

Who doesn't want to be around others who listen, care, and offer help when needed? We all do. While seeking such a friendship, strive to become that type of friend.

Look in the Mirror

If your friend is hurt, does it hurt your heart also? Offer to do something instead of waiting to be asked. Often, people won't ask for help. Being emotionally wounded, spiritually drained, and physically tired leaves little energy for thinking of specific tasks. If you don't know what to say or do, be present.

Prayer

Dear God, thank you for the blessing of friendship. Help me to honor this relationship by responding with a loving heart that's moved to action. Amen.

Clear the Air

"To handle yourself, use your head; to handle others, use your heart."
—Eleanor Roosevelt

Sherry wrapped a cape around Gail's neck. "Sorry, but I'm out of robes."

Gail was used to getting a cape and a short robe to protect her clothing. She glanced around the packed salon. Seeing that the robes were all in use, she shrugged.

During the color application, Sherry's fingers flicked against Gail's blouse where the cape was open in the back. When Gail removed her top at home, she spotted a small spot of hair dye. She mentioned it at her next appointment. Sherry offered laundry suggestions. Gail let it go since Sherry always did a great job on color.

Gail returned in two months for a root touch-up. When Sherry handed her a mirror, her eyes widened. Her hair was a bright, brassy orange. "It looks like fire's coming out of my head. This isn't *my* color."

"That shade didn't arrive with the order, so I tried something different."

Gail insisted on a correction, which took three hours and exposure to another chemical treatment. After a couple more incidents, Gail had suffered enough. She tried calling Sherry several times. Her requests for a call back went unanswered. Finally, she sent a text stating her disappointments and that she wouldn't be returning. Sherry sent a couple of texts, inquiring about Gail's wellbeing, but avoided the issues.

Sometimes, a stylist must initiate a hard conversation. Tawanda had honored a new client's wishes for months. The woman was never satisfied. Finally, Tawanda said, "I'm not doing the job as you'd like. That saddens me. So, it would be best if you found another stylist."

It can be difficult to express disappointment or to hear you've let someone down. God understands that and provides guidance on how to handle conflict. "If a fellow believer hurts you, go and tell him—work it out between the two of you. If he listens, you've made a friend" (Matthew 18:15, MSG).

Two of the early Christian evangelists Paul and Barnabas disagreed about Barnabas' desire to take along his cousin John Mark. Paul was against the idea because John Mark had abandoned them on a prior missionary journey. Paul and Barnabas separated and each continued to preach, spreading the gospel in two paths (Acts 15:36-39). Later, John Mark wrote the gospel of Mark and became part of Paul's ministry.

Acknowledging someone's feelings can be a big step toward clearing the air, even if the conflict can't be resolved. We can disagree agreeably. Keep the conflict private. Even if the conflict can't be resolved, an amicable parting might pave the way for later reconciliation.

Look in the Mirror

Are you experiencing conflict with someone? Have you tried to resolve the matter? Have you listened to understand and not just be heard? Have you done as much as you can? If so, let the matter rest and keep your heart open for reconciliation.

Prayer

Dear God, I don't want to be in conflict. Show me if there's something I can do. Once I've done my part, help me to be at peace within myself. Amen.

Flames of Fire

"I get angry about things, then go on and work."
—Toni Morrison

My scalp usually began itching a week before a relaxer appointment. I often forgot about the upcoming appointment and gave my scalp a good scratch. Sweet relief! I wouldn't give it another thought until the beautician applied the chemical straightener.

Aaaggghhh! My scalp felt as if it was on fire. I wanted to jump out of the chair and dunk my head in a tub of water. Or even in a toilet bowl as Denzel Washington did, trying to wash "conk" out of his hair in the movie *Malcolm X*. Anything to cool the flame. Why does the relaxer burn so much?

The active ingredient in relaxers (also, conk from the 1920s-1960s) is sodium hydroxide, a caustic chemical a.k.a. "lye." It can penetrate the skin and cause irritation, even chemical burns. Similarly, harsh words go deep, damaging the mind and spirit. Whether hurled in anger, scribbled on paper, or pounded on a keyboard, words have power.

Jesus' half-brother, James, devotes almost an entire chapter on the words we speak, referring to our tongue. He likens it to several small, but powerful things: a bit in a horse's mouth, able to control this huge animal; a tiny rudder capable of turning a huge ship facing strong winds; a spark, which can set a great forest on fire. He compares the tongue to flames, a blaze capable of destroying life (James 3:2-7).

Our words reflect what's inside our hearts. "Out of the same mouth come praise and cursing. My brothers and sisters, this should not be" (James 3:10, NIV). Words can be used as a tool to build up (life) or to tear down (death).

Proverbs 18:21 teaches that the power of life and death is in our words. Don't wield them as weapons of destruction by lashing out at others. Rather, garnish the power of the Holy Spirit, which gives us power to control our words.

Look in the Mirror

An African proverb says: "Words are like spears: Once they leave your lips they can never come back." Picture yourself holding the spear. Imagine your words as the tip. Think of the damage that'll be done if the spear is thrown. Would you still hurl it? If you've been on the receiving end of harsh words, and have suffered wounds, ask the Holy Spirit to help heal you.

Prayer

Dear Holy Spirit, help me with the words that come out of my mouth. Since you live inside me, hate and hurt cannot co-exist. I pray to speak words that will not offend, and I ask you to heal scars from words that have wounded me. Amen.

Listen Well

"The best listeners listen between the lines."
—Nina Malkin

Awakened by the knock on the door, Cynthia stumbled groggily down the steps. She opened the door to our neighbor Carla. "Sorry it took so long. I was taking a nap."

"I can tell." Carla grinned, pointing to Cynthia's hair. "Your hair looks nappy."

Cynthia could barely follow the rest of the conversation with Carla, who is Caucasian. *How dare she call my hair nappy?* Cynthia was still mulling over the comment when she spotted me working in my yard and told me about the exchange. "Do you think Carla was trying to insult me?"

"Maybe she doesn't know that 'nappy' is a derogatory term. Besides, you straighten your hair."

A few minutes later, Carla pulled into her driveway. She parked her car and walked over to us. "Hey, guys. What's up?"

Cynthia shared a glance with me before turning to Carla. "Remember what you said about my hair?"

"Oh, yeah. It looked nappy. One side of your hair was flat from lying down. Nappy." She brought her hands together and leaned her head on top of them, smashing her hair. When we didn't return her smile, she asked, "Did I say something wrong?"

We educated her that the term was often used as an insult. Carla didn't know that her comment fell just short of take-off-your-earrings-and-get-ready-to-fight words. Cynthia and I realized that our friend hadn't intended her comment as anything but an observation, not a slight.

Talking things over helps to understand others' motivations and prevents developing a wedge in relationships.

After the Israelites divided territories in the Promised Land, two of the tribes began building a large altar. Their fellow tribesmen assumed the altar was for an idol. Before waging war, they sent a delegation to determine what these tribes could be thinking.

The tribesmen declared, "The Lord, the Mighty One, is God! He knows the truth, and may Israel know it, too! We have not built the altar in treacherous rebellion against the Lord" (Joshua 22:22, NLT). That ended all talk of war.

In the scripture written by James, he advises us to be quick to listen but slow to speak or get angry (James 1:19). Many misunderstandings can be prevented by not assuming the worst and taking time to listen.

Look in the Mirror

Are you quick to become angry or annoyed and tell somebody off? Write what you are feeling and would like to say. Take some time to cool off and not speak in the heat of the moment. Sleep on what you think you understand. Before saying anything, ask for clarification.

Prayer

Father God, I don't want to walk around offended. Help me to be willing to listen and allow my heart to be open to understanding. Amen.

Share Good News

"If you have knowledge, let others light their candles in it."
—Margaret Fuller

Spotting Debra in the women's locker room, I tried to avoid letting my gaze linger on her shaved head. *Could it be cancer? I wonder if she's all right.* She didn't appear ill. In fact, she looked fit and trim following her personal training sessions.

I worked up the nerve to approach her. "I don't want to be insulting. Your hair suits you, and you wear it well. But, are you okay?"

"I'm fine," she said with a grin. "Remember when I had long locks?" She reached into her locker and pulled out her employee I.D. Several years old, it pictured her with locks hanging to the middle of her back. "I shaved them off."

I popped my fingers. *Snap.* "Just like that?"

"Yep. Something in me knew it was the right time to go for it. I've never looked back." She eyed my hair. "Hair is work, even locks. I'm glad to be free of the hassle of working my hair."

Debra had immediately known when it was time to give up working her old hairstyle and to embrace the freedom her new look offered. When we accept Jesus' message of grace, we are called to tell others about the freedom we experience.

The Bible tells the story of Jesus' first disciples who followed him at once. James and his brother John and another set of brothers, Simon (later called Peter) and Andrew, were professional fishermen. They were in their boats when Jesus called to them to "fish for people." They left their jobs and followed Jesus (Matthew 4:18-22).

Later in scripture, Jesus talks about the sacrifices some of his disciples made, such as leaving their homes and families. He provided assurance that his followers will receive much more in this life and in eternity (Luke 18:29-30).

Does that mean we won't have trouble? No, we all do. But when we accept Jesus' invitation to follow him, we have a relationship with him with its many blessings. No one can out-give God, beginning with resting from the burden of having to work for salvation. "Learn the unforced rhythms of grace. I won't lay anything heavy or ill-fitting on you" (Matthew 11:30, MSG).

Considering the demands certain hairstyles make, we sometimes give them up. We share how our lives are made easier. How much more should we be willing to tell others about Jesus' love? Not everyone is called to be an evangelist, but simply offer a word of encouragement and tell others about Jesus' goodness.

Look in the Mirror

When was the last time you had to walk away from a commitment that had become burdensome? How did you feel once you made a choice? Did you tell others about the action you took or how proud you felt? Don't underestimate how your story of freedom in Christ could change someone's life.

Prayer

Dear Jesus, thank you for asking me to share the good news of my faith, that I don't have to work to be free from eternal death. Help me to share this freedom with others. Amen.

Show Respect

"I got exhausted with constantly saying to people,
'Don't touch. Thanks for the compliment,
but keep your hands to yourself.'"
—Mena Fombo

Textured hair sparks a lot of curiosity. Sometimes, I want to answer questions with how I might be thinking.

"Is that your hair?"

It's mine, even if I bought it.

"Can you wash it?"

Like with shampoo? Have you ever heard of it?

"Can I touch your hair?"

I am not a pet!

An acquaintance embraced me during the church "meet-and-greet." Her hand shifted to my hair and her fingers stroked my locks. I pulled back and glared at her. "Why are you touching my hair like that?"

"It feels so different."

"But I don't go around touching your hair!"

Heads turned at the sound of my raised voice. Later, I considered how to handle the encounter differently. Sometimes it's hard not to take offense. However, Jesus wants us to practice tolerance and to treat others with grace.

Someone tried a stealth touch on him. A crowd was pressing him when a woman who had suffered twelve years with a bleeding disorder touched his cloak. Jesus called her out. "Who touched my clothes?" This touch was different because he felt healing power flow from him. She stepped forward and admitted to her desperation. Jesus told her to go in peace as she'd been healed because of her faith (Luke 8:42-48). He knew her motive and her heart.

The woman hugging me hadn't come for healing. Instead of yelling, I could've offered a loving rebuke, such as, "I don't like it when my hair is touched without permission." If anyone asks before touching, I can offer a simple, "No." Words spoken in kindness can often get the point across rather than losing our head to the moment.

Look in the Mirror

Perhaps you've been the victim of an unwanted touch to your hair or a bold hand aiming straight at your head. You can respond with, "Please, don't touch my hair." If asked to touch your hair, offer a sweet, "No, I don't like my hair to be touched."

Prayer

Jesus, help me to remember that I'm accountable for how I respond. I pray to speak with a spirit of kindness, even when I say, "No."

Look Beyond the Surface

"... A person speculated about who I was as a person and even read into my personal life based solely off my hairstyle. He or she said I must be lazy because I have short hair. It was just devastating."
—Tamron Hall

I spotted a bottle of shea butter conditioner tucked between my co-worker's laptop and desk organizer. I pointed to it. "That's what I use on my hair. Do you put that on yours?"

Karen picked up the partially used bottle. "Yes. The consultant at the beauty supply store recommended it after my permanent." She scrunched her light-brown, super-fine hair. "She said it would help relax the curl and put the moisture back."

Some products can be applied to anyone's hair. It does not matter whether it sits atop a face with white skin and vibrant green eyes like Karen or one with mocha skin and rich chocolate brown irises like mine. The same is true of the Gospel of Jesus Christ.

Acts 10:9-12 tells the story of the apostle Peter, who fell into a trance while praying. In his vision, he saw a large sheet from heaven being lowered. It contained all kinds of animals, including reptiles and birds considered off-limits by Jewish people. When a voice commanded Peter to rise and eat, he refused. "I've never even tasted anything that was impure or unclean." Despite his hunger and three assurances that the food was okay, Peter still refused the feast.

As Peter sat wondering what the vision meant, three men came to the door. They wanted him to travel with them to the home of a Gentile, a person of another culture.

Peter accompanied them to Cornelius' house. He shared his vision of an angel telling him to ask for Peter.

Then Peter understood the visions he and Cornelius received. God accepts everyone regardless of race. Once Peter shared the message of Jesus' life, death, and resurrection, all of Cornelius' household believed in Jesus. Then they began speaking in another language.

Peter declared, "They've received the Holy Spirit exactly as we did" (Acts 10:47).

Hair products are topical applications—regardless of the skin color to which it's applied. The message of salvation is more than skin deep and has the power to penetrate deep into the soul.

Look in the Mirror

Do you make judgments about others based on appearance? Consider what might be driving your feelings. Think about God's view that all people are the same in his eyes and worthy of his love and acceptance.

Prayer

God, thank you for seeing beyond superficial differences like skin color. Your son died for everyone's sins, regardless of race or culture. Let me see others with a loving heart. Amen.

Rise by Lifting Others

"The success of every woman should be the inspiration to another. We should raise each other up..."
—Serena Williams

My beautician handed me a new price sheet. "The salon's prices are changing based on the level of certification. Since I'm a master stylist, I'll be paid the higher rate."

I stared at the prices and swallowed. "I've paid the same price every two weeks for the last year. Now, it'll double?"

Marge lifted her palms. "It's out of my hands."

As she shampooed my hair, my thoughts bounced back and forth. My budget would take a big hit if I stayed. However, the salon was less than five minutes from my home. I liked Marge's work. How could she think I would stand for this? Undecided, I left without making another appointment.

Once home, I prayed about how to resolve the matter and realized Marge was only doing her job. She worked for the salon, which set the prices. Then it hit me. *What if I remained at the salon but chose another stylist performing the same services?*

I called the salon and after asking about other stylists' prices, requested to be booked with Sheila. Her prices were lower than what I'd been paying, plus she was able to give me the early morning appointment I preferred. One issue concerned me: Sheila and Marge were good friends.

I squirmed when Marge saw me sitting in Sheila's chair. "Good morning," I said, expecting a cool response.

Marge greeted me warmly and took a seat in the chair where I normally sat when she serviced me. Rather than reacting with anger or jealousy, she seemed happy for her friend to have gotten a new client and for the salon to have kept a customer. Soon, the three of us chatted as if I'd always been Sheila's client. Stepping aside for another person's advancement or ministry doesn't have to be a source of irritation or jealousy.

John the Baptist's popularity was growing. But when Jesus began teaching, more people flocked to him. John's disciples complained. "Rabbi, that man who was with you on the other side of the Jordan—the one you testified about—look, he is baptizing, and everyone is going to him" (John 3:26, NIV). Jealousy had blinded them to the Messiah's arrival. They only saw their shrinking ministry.

John knew that God had given him specific work: Point people to Jesus. "He must become greater and greater, and I must become less and less" (John 3: 30).

We don't have to resent others' advancements. When it seems your grip is slipping, hold onto the truth. What God has for you is just for you. Our work is serving the one who called us, and not our own interests.

Look in the Mirror

Think about the last time an acquaintance received a blessing. How did you react? Did you offer "congratulations"? Or, did you think about some lack in your life? Look for ways to celebrate another's success and still maintain a good attitude.

Prayer

Dear God, help me to focus on you. I don't want to become distracted, disturbed, or dismayed by another's success. Show me how to be faithful to what you've given me to do. Amen.

Recognize Tangled Relationships

"Her hair was NOT going to show in the store ...
That was because Joe never told Janie how jealous he
was. He never told her how often he had seen
other men figuratively wallowing in it..."
—*Their Eyes Were Watching God*, Zora Neale Thurston

I approached the attendant at my church's guest services desk. "I think I forgot my umbrella last week."

The man stepped from behind the counter and jerked his head. "Let's go take a look in the lost and found closet." As we walked, he glanced at my hair. "Nice locks." He ran a hand over his bald head. "I miss mine. But I shaved them off."

"Why would you do that if you liked them so much?"

"The woman I was dating became jealous when other women complimented me."

"Are you still with her?"

He shook his head. "Nope. I broke it off. She was trying to control me." He smiled at me. "I think I'll start my locks again."

Unlike the attendant who quickly ended his relationship, some of us find it difficult to cut someone out of our life—even when remaining together threatens our identity.

While the Old Testament judge, Samson, loved Delilah, she "played him" for money. Two times, she tied him with ropes so that other men, hidden in the room, could attack him. Despite Delilah's betrayals, Samson wouldn't break off the relationship.

Her daily nagging wore him down. "Delilah lulled Samson to sleep with his head in her lap, and then she called in a man to shave off the seven locks of his hair. In this way she began to bring him down, and his strength left him" (Judges 16:19, NLT).

We can become lost in our relationships, whether it be a partner, family member, or even a co-worker or boss. The list is endless. We must wake up to the reality that sometimes another's love is rooted in control or a motive that isn't in our best interests.

Christ offers us a place and purpose that is not controlling but loving. We will never lose, including our identity, when we put our trust in him.

Look in the Mirror

Take stock of your relationships. Are there any that make you feel inferior or controlled? Ask yourself why you're staying. Have you become a prisoner of your emotions? Ask God for the strength to break off any unhealthy relationships. If you feel that your safety is at risk, a counselor or other resources can help protect you.

Prayer

Heavenly Father, help me to recognize unhealthy relationships. I don't want to lose myself in anyone. Please give me the courage to make a change, even when it's difficult. Amen.

Jealousy … Be Gone!

"Be thankful for what you have; you'll end up having more. If you concentrate on what you don't have, you will never, ever have enough."
—Oprah Winfrey

"Yeah, I can work you in," your stylist speaks into her cell phone. "Let me check my schedule." She shoves the flat iron into the heater stove before lightly touching your shoulder. "This will only take a sec."

Steam rises from your head. It's not from the hot tools being used on your hair. *No, she didn't just tell somebody she could come in at the last minute! A walk-in?* You made your appointment weeks ago and arrived on time—even a little early.

The stylist doesn't seem to realize the person on the phone is taking time which could be spent styling your hair. "Okay, I'll see you in an hour." She hangs up, gives you a smile, and tries to engage in conversation. Meanwhile, you're still talking to yourself.

The cut wasn't so great the last time. And the color wasn't worth what she charged. Maybe it's time to consider looking elsewhere.

When feelings of injustice surface, we might simmer in silence or walk away in anger. Jesus wants us to appreciate that his grace is as much for others as it is for us.

The men in Matthew 20:12 had agreed to work in a vineyard all day for a specific salary. Others were hired an hour before quitting time—for the same pay as those who started in the morning. They complained to the manager. "These last workers put in only one easy hour, and you just made them equal to us."

Jesus asked why they felt angry. "Don't I have the right to do what I want with my own money? Or are you envious because I am generous?" (Matthew 20:15, NIV).

Although the Bible doesn't give their response, we can imagine their thinking, *That's not fair*! So, why did their attitude deteriorate? They had been thankful until they started making comparisons, which demand superiority or inferiority.

So, what if someone is good to another? It doesn't take anything away from what we've been promised. God's blessings don't have a maximum capacity level, so they never run out.

Look in the Mirror

Do you feel hostility when you think someone has gotten a break that you didn't? Try counting your blessings as if ticking off your ABCs. Pick a letter from the alphabet and list a blessing associated with it: H - "I'm grateful for the *home* I live in." I – "I'm grateful for *inspiration* in finding a way to style my hair." By the time you go through the alphabet, thankfulness will fill the space once occupied by envy or jealousy.

Prayer

God, help me not to get caught up in comparing my portion to another's. I pray to be thankful for what you've provided and to trust that you have blessings stored up just for me. Amen.

DEALING WITH DIFFICULT CIRCUMSTANCES

"My mission in life is not merely to survive, but to thrive; and to do so with some passion, some compassion, some humor, and some style."
—Maya Angelou

Count the Cost

"The thing about doing anything artificial to your hair is that you have to look after it."
—Francesca Annis

"Mom, why can't I have blue hair?" Jennifer ran her fingers through her dark strands before letting the tresses fall free. "Brown is so boring. Some girls are even going purple. Besides, I'll be eighteen next week."

Having debated with her teenage daughter for several months, Becky made a decision. "You have to pay for it."

Jennifer engulfed her in a big hug. "Thanks, Mom! This is going to be so cool." Jennifer saved money from extra chores and babysitting. Although she'd only be able to afford *four* blue streaks, it didn't dampen her excitement.

The stylist bleached several sections of Jennifer's hair before applying the long-desired color. Afterward, Jennifer studied herself in the mirror. She leaned toward the lights, angling her head back and forth. "I can hardly see any blue," she said with a disappointing voice.

The stylist used her fingers to tick off the maintenance requirements. "Bleach dries out the hair, so you'll need special conditioners. Cut back on blow-drying. Absolutely no swimming. Chlorine will remove the color and you'll have blonde streaks."

Upon hearing the maintenance required, combined with giving up swimming, her favorite summer activity, Jennifer burst into tears. "I hate blonde!"

Coloring hair is more than just a cosmetic enhancement. There are things we must research, such as possible damage and the investment—dollars and time—to maintain the look. We must be careful about considering only what we want to hear and ignoring negative information.

In the Bible, when the Israelites demanded a king, Samuel, one of the Old Testament judges, cautioned them. His warnings included their sons being drafted, their daughters forced to cook and bake, and taxes levied on their property (1 Samuel 8:10-17). When Samuel's warnings came true, the people wanted relief. Some decisions have far-reaching consequences. Scripture reminds us that we are to consider the costs before we act (Luke 14:28-30).

Coloring hair does not have as long-lasting effects as some decisions, but we can feel burdened. God wants us to consider all the implications before we leap.

Look in the Mirror

Are you weighing a decision? Make a list of positives and negatives. Include both tangible costs like money and intangibles like time. Ask questions. Take your time. Seek wise counsel and mentoring if necessary.

Prayer

God, I pray not to rush into anything but weigh all the consequences. Please open my mind and heart to all information. Amen.

In the Valley of Despair and Loss

"As I walk through the valley of hair loss I will not fear, for as my hair falls, I know I am stronger—I will know I am more than my hair…"
—WomensHairLossProject

My sister, Audrey, lay in bed, exhausted after another round of chemotherapy for treating breast cancer. I brushed her hair, and although my strokes were gentle, her hair crumbled as if fried to a crisp. I set the brush aside and used my fingers. Clumps of her hair covered my fingers and palms. Tears filled our eyes as we stared at the nest of brittle strands.

"Go ahead," she said. "Just cut it off."

I found a pair of scissors and began snipping. A question came to my mind with each snip. *How could this have happened? Why would God allow a disease to strike one of his faithful children? Why wouldn't God take the disease away?*

God showed he was always present. Audrey had switched beauticians a few months before her diagnosis. When she was diagnosed with cancer, she learned her new beautician styled wigs. Audrey now works at a cancer treatment center helping others who fight the disease.

When sickness strikes, we cry out with questions for God. He responds by assuring us that he does hear us and is also with us. Our questions diminish as we become assured of his presence and care, like sheep travelling through a valley. They require great care from the shepherd to make it through.

Psalm 23 in the Bible records the psalmist David's experience as a shepherd. He took sheep through valleys on the way to high country. In the valleys, green meadows nourished the sheep and cool streams of water refreshed them. They had a chance to rest and become rejuvenated.

The valley is part of the path to higher ground. So what if the journey leads to death? Let's face it. Life is uncertain, yet death brings a promise for those who have trusted in Christ. *I will live in the house of the Lord forever* (Psalm 23:6). Our Good Shepherd offers eternal comfort, whether he brings us to the mountaintop in this life or the other side.

We'd rather not travel the deepest, darkest parts of life's valleys. Uncertainty looms over us like a huge rocky mountain. We are comforted by a shepherd who provides his presence. There will be valleys for all of us. But for the sheep of God's pasture, we can trust him to comfort us as we walk together.

Look in the Mirror

Are you struggling with an illness? Pay attention to what your body is telling you. Is it calling for rest? Are you receiving proper nourishment? Connect with others who have gone through the same experience. Ask God to guide you through this, no matter where he leads.

Prayer

Lord, you are the Great Shepherd. I am a sheep in your pasture. You hear my voice, even when it's filled with questions. I am trusting you to guide me through this valley. Amen.

Handling Embarrassing Situations

"You can't control everything—your hair was put on your head to remind you of that."
—Anonymous

***W**ham!* Sharon's car jerked forward when another vehicle plowed into hers from behind. Her mind raced. *Call the police. Take photos. Exchange names.* She slid the gearshift into park and hurried to inspect the damage. Her almost new car sported a crumpled bumper and a dented trunk.

The other driver approached, studying her with a curious stare. "Are you okay?"

"I think so. I need to get a pen and paper out of the car." Bending down to reach inside, she caught a glimpse of herself in the mirror—wearing only a stocking cap. Through the window, she glimpsed the wig sitting on her dashboard.

Embarrassment warmed her cheeks and anger rose inside her. She took a deep breath and uttered a quick prayer. "Holy Spirit, help me to stay calm." A feeling of peace washed over her. After one final breath, she opened the car door, snatched the wig off its perch, and plopped it onto her head. Then, she walked back to the driver and calmly obtained his insurance information before the police arrived.

Controlling our emotions in trying circumstances may be difficult, but it's not impossible with the Holy Spirit's help. Two of Jesus' closest friends, John and his brother James, struggled in this area.

Known as the "Sons of Thunder" for their zeal and fiery preaching, they were sent to Samaria to prepare for Jesus' arrival. The Samaritans didn't want anything to do with Jesus. When the brothers reported what had happened, they wanted lightning to strike the Samaritans

(Luke 9:54). As part of Jesus' inner circle, we expect they could control their temper!

Allowing the Holy Spirit to control our emotions doesn't happen overnight. Over time, God smooths our rough edges. Jesus reminded them that their manner was not like the spirit of God. The Holy Spirit exemplifies behaviors such as gentleness and self-control (Galatians 5:22). The brothers took Jesus' teaching to heart, and rather than exacting revenge, they traveled to another village to continue spreading the gospel of Jesus Christ. In time, the Holy Spirit brought their tempers under control.

Once we accept Christ as our Savior, we immediately receive God's spirit. However, it takes time and prayer to allow his spirit to guide us in handling difficult, embarrassing, and unexpected circumstances.

Look in the Mirror

How did you handle a high-stress situation? If you were not loving, diplomatic, or if your emotions were all over the place, consider what you can do the next time. You might take deep breaths before reacting. Say a few words in prayer. "I have the spirit of peace… of love… of self-control…" When you feel a decrease in heart rate and pulse, then speak and act knowing God's spirit is working in you.

Prayer

Holy Spirit, I'm in a tough spot. I need your help. Guide me in how to speak and how to act. Amen.

Change Your Perspective

"So, you don't want to change the color and you don't want to go shorter and you don't want extensions but you're ready for a whole new look... um okay."
—Anonymous

"I want my hair to look like this." Audrey showed her beautician the dog-eared photo of the actress Halle Barry, with her iconic pixie cut. "Except, I don't want it quite as short and keep the bangs longer to sweep over my forehead."

After the shampoo and blow-dry, the stylist combed and snipped for another forty minutes. "How do you like it?"

Audrey studied her hair from different angles, tilting her head, left and right, up and down. "It's all right. But it doesn't look like the picture."

Over the next several months, her stylist worked to create a style that highlighted Audrey's best features. The result—which Audrey loved—was shorter than the picture she had admired.

We may not carry an actual photo that shows what our expected "after" looks like, but we often hold a mental image of a hopeful outcome. However, our perspective is limited. God wants us to open ourselves to his eternal plan and trust him for the result.

One Bible story tells how Naomi traveled to Moab with her husband and two sons to escape the famine in their homeland, Bethlehem. Her husband died shortly after moving, leaving Naomi a single parent. Her sons grew up and married. Ten years later, both sons died about the same time.

Naomi decided to go back to Bethlehem since the famine had ended. Heading out with her daughters-in-law, Ruth and Orpah, Naomi urged them to go home to their mothers. She thought God was working against her (Ruth 1:13). But God planned to reveal a blessing she never imagined.

Ruth insisted on coming with Naomi. They arrived in town at the beginning of the harvest. Ruth worked the fields for a wealthy man named Boaz, one of Naomi's closest relatives. He made sure the women were provided for physically. By the end of the harvest, Boaz married Ruth. Naomi cared for their child, who was an ancestor of Jesus Christ, our Lord and Savior.

As situations and circumstances change, we must adjust our perspective. God's vision included a plan for eternal salvation. His focus is beyond what we can visualize. When we let go of the picture in our mind, he will reveal his vision for us that's far beyond what we could ever imagine!

Look in the Mirror

Perhaps you're facing change in your life. It might be your choice, like a hairstyle. Maybe it's outside of your control, like a job lay-off, a family move, or switching to a new school. Let go of the notion that the road to your destiny must look a certain way. Trust God to lead you on a path that is likely different than what you envisioned. When he reveals the outcome, you'll agree that it was far better than you imagined.

Prayer

God, I have thoughts and dreams about my life and how to achieve them. Help me to release them to you. I trust you to work out your vision for my life and your eternal purposes. Amen.

Curing What Ails You

"Faith and prayer are the vitamins of the soul; man cannot live in health without them."
—Mahalia Jackson

Tears filled my eyes and threatened to spill down my cheeks. "This stuff stinks." If a product didn't smell bad, my parents didn't think it worked.

Mama pressed her lips. "It'll help your hair grow and your scalp to stop itching."

"But, isn't 'dog mange' for dogs?"

She pointed toward her bedroom. "You better bring my comb and sit down so I can do your hair."

I ran to the bedroom, grabbed the big-toothed comb, and plopped on the floor at her feet. She parted my hair before dipping her index finger into the jar, scooping out a dab of foul-smelling goo, and smearing it onto my scalp. Within a few weeks, the itch was gone. The salve's active ingredients, sulfur and pine tar, do help "mangy" dogs that lose their fur. It also works on human scalps.

Some unusual treatments are passed down through generations, like swallowing turpentine and sugar for colds—one of my father's favorites. Please don't try this at home, or anywhere! There are other natural remedies, such as using burnt flour to treat diaper rash or blisters. Scripture records some odd ingredients used in Jesus' miracles.

The most powerful ingredient was *faith* in his ability to heal followed by action. To heal a blind man, Jesus spat on the ground, made mud with his saliva, and smoothed it over the man's eyes. Jesus told him to wash in the pool of Siloam. The man did as he was told and was able to see (John 9:6-7). Ten lepers cried to Jesus for mercy. He told them to show themselves to the priests. As they went, their leprosy disappeared (Luke 17:11-14). However, when prayers for healing seem to go unanswered, our faith is challenged.

Sometimes Jesus uses people with an affliction to bring about the ultimate good: spreading the good news that he has power over death. At Lazarus's grave, he asked Martha, the dead man's sister, "Didn't I tell you that you will see God's glory if you believe?" (John 11:38-40, NLT). They rolled the stone aside, and after praying to God, Jesus shouted for Lazarus to come out of the grave.

Jesus doesn't want our hearts to be hard and stony because of affliction. He wants us to exercise faith so that no matter what happens, the cure for the consummate illness—death—can be ours through him.

Look in the Mirror

What's in your medicine or kitchen cabinet? Any "natural" cures? Do you read labels, hoping there are more ingredients you can pronounce versus chemicals? If you can place faith in a manmade or natural product, believe in Jesus, our source of healing.

Prayer

Lord, when sickness strikes, I want to get well. Thank you for medicine and for providing knowledge to the doctors. You are the ultimate physician and the source of all healing. So, I place my faith in you. Amen.

Holding Onto Peace

"When a train goes through a tunnel and it gets dark,
you don't throw away the ticket and jump off.
You sit still and trust the engineer."
—Corrie Ten Boom

"I'm cutting Macy's hair off!" Gloria's high-pitched screams through the phone were loud enough to turn heads in office cubicles. "I can't get it out."

"Wait! Wait!" Joe urged his mother-in-law. He imagined the things a three-year-old could put in her hair. *Gum? Paint? Glue?* "What can't you get out?"

Gloria wailed. "Putty!" She sobbed. "I was in the kitchen. She was with Grandpa. He ran upstairs for a few minutes. When I found her…" She gave one final sniff. "I'm getting the scissors." She hung up before Joe could respond.

Grabbing his car keys, he fled the office. He gunned his car out of the parking lot, sped to his in-laws, and raced into the house. "Where is she?"

The grandparents led him to the bedroom. Sure enough, a section of Macy's hair had been cut. She was curled up on the bed, sound asleep, oblivious to her father's labored breathing or the anxious stares of her grandparents.

A tear rolled down Gloria's cheek. "She bawled when I cut her hair."

Joe's father-in-law added, "She didn't start crying until you got upset. Once you calmed down, so did she. Sleeping like a baby." Later, the family found other options for handling the messy situation.

When storms arise, we often panic. Jesus wants us to trust him when life's problems seem overwhelming.

Late one evening, Jesus told his disciples to climb into a boat and cross over to the other side of a lake. The fierce storm brought high waves, filling the boat with water. The disciples, experienced fishermen, panicked. They yelled, "Teacher, don't you care that we're going to drown?" (Mark 4:38). Yet, they had Jesus, the Prince of Peace with them (Isaiah 6:9).

Jesus, sleeping in the back of the boat, awoke and rebuked the wind and told the waves to be still. He knows the storms we'll face.

Scripture tells us to give our worries to God because he cares for us (1 Peter 5:7). The Psalmist David wrote that he was able to lie down and sleep and wake up in safety because the Lord was watching over him (Psalm 3:5). When we focus on Jesus, who calms the storm in us, we sleep as soundly as a baby.

Look in the Mirror

Does it seem that circumstances beyond your control are crashing on you like waves? Do you toss and turn, unable to sleep? Tell the Lord what is troubling you. Rest in promises such as, "Weeping may last through the night, but joy comes with the morning" (Psalm 30:5). Recite the verses until you feel Jesus' peace settle you.

Prayer

Dear Lord, this situation is beyond anything I can do. But I know that you have power over everything. Awaken my trust in you. Calm the storm in me. Amen.

Learning to Wait

"I've been praying to Jesus and Holy Ghost for patience and have also mentioned that it would help if I didn't have frizzy hair."
—Margaret Sartor

Marsha's voice was a whisper. "Hey, what's up, girl?"

"It sounds like you're in the basement," I said.

"I'm in a hallway, waiting for a chair inside the shop to free up."

Marsha sets aside a minimum of five hours when she goes to the salon. The shop holds three people. Her beautician might be flat-ironing one client's hair. Another customer could be sleeping under a dryer while a third receives a conditioning treatment. While the beautician works, she cradles a cell phone to her ear and talks to a friend about the weekly drama playing on the big screen TV. When the beautician's daughter drops by, they discuss the guest list for a wedding reception, which prolongs Marsha's appointment.

Asked why she remains a customer, Marsha responded, "I've been with her for years and she knows my hair." She feels the results are worth the wait.

I, on the other hand, have walked out of a beauty or barber shop after twenty minutes of waiting. My unwillingness to wait is not confined to the beauty salon. It extends to other areas of my life. I've rushed into things I later regretted, such as jobs, major purchases, and relationships. God says he knows what we need and if we wait for him, there are more and better things than if we plow ahead on our own.

The patriarch of the Christian faith, Abraham was 100 when he had a son through his wife, Sarah, who was ninety. They were told to name him Isaac, meaning "he laughs" (Genesis 21:2-7). Moses killed a man and then spent forty years in exile until God transformed him into a leader (Acts 7:23-30). David was anointed king when he was a youth but didn't take the throne until he was thirty years old (2 Samuel 5:4). I'm sure they would all agree that the results were worth the wait.

Waiting on God isn't easy. We might be tempted to think he doesn't understand what we're going through. Or that the delay is an invitation for us to jump in—quickly. Rather than pressing ahead, God might be using the time to transform our character. He might be calling us to a time of rest and renewal. Perhaps the timing is not right to give us what we have requested. Or he might have something better.

God fulfills his promises, which are wonderfully good to those who wait for him and seek him (Lamentations 3:24).

Look in the Mirror

What are some of the things for which you are waiting? Identify at least one thing you can see and give thanks for today. Do this daily until you have an answer. Your situation might not change, but you will.

Prayer

God, show me how to wait. During this time of preparation, I pray to know you in a deeper way. Help increase my trust in you. Amen.

Saying Good-bye

"Every day is a new day, and you'll never be able to find happiness if you don't move on."
—Carrie Underwood

It was a pleasure having you as a client, but as of today, I no longer work at the salon.

I snapped wide awake reading my stylist's 6:30 a.m. text. I responded, *Hope you're o.k.* Hoping that Michelle could be persuaded to do my hair, I sent another message. "Are you going to be doing hair anywhere else?"

She responded with an unequivocal *No*.

I could hardly believe I would be on the hunt for another stylist after only one year. How long would it take to find someone else? Would she be as timely and creative? Would we get along as well? Michelle and I had shared thoughts on hair, faith, and even dating. While it felt as if I was losing a friend, I also felt angry over her unexpected, sudden departure.

Denial, bargaining, and anger—three of the five stages of mourning. God understands we must process a loss, until we finally accept it, before we can receive the new thing he is doing.

Peter had just realized that Jesus was the promised Messiah. Then Jesus began telling his disciples that he was going to Jerusalem to suffer before being killed. Peter freaked. *What happened to getting the keys of the Kingdom of Heaven? Didn't you just call me "the rock upon which the church would be built?"*

Peter took Jesus aside and scolded him. "Heaven forbid, Lord," he said. "This will never happen to you" (Matthew 16:22). Peter was upset because he wanted Jesus to rule on earth.

But God was doing something new. Jesus' mission was to suffer and die for the sins of the world so that his followers could experience a new and better life. Jesus told Peter, "You are seeing things merely from a human point of view, not from God's" (Matthew 16:23).

God doesn't want us to stay stuck in yesterday's sorrow. "Forget the former things; do not dwell on the past. See, I am doing a new thing!" (Isaiah 43:18-19, NIV). Could it be that someone in your life has a destiny to fulfill? Believe it for *your* life. Let the promise of restoration take root and spring forth with new blessings.

Look in the Mirror

Have you suffered the loss of a relationship? Grief isn't confined only to physical death. It could be the loss of a job, a home, and even what you hoped for in life. Any of these can cause us to mourn. Recognize the stages: denial, anger, bargaining, depression, acceptance. You may not experience them all, in sequence, or only once. Allow yourself to grieve. Gradually, you will get to acceptance and eventually, the celebration of your new life.

Prayer

Dear God, letting go is hard. Your word says that even Jesus wept. Although tears come, I'm reminded that you keep them in your bottle. As I walk through this loss, I will believe in your promise of restoration. Amen.

Revealing Secrets

"I have been struggling with hair loss for most of my adult life ... I am not alone in this and my goal is to help others while at the same time unshackle myself from this quiet hell I have been living in ..."
—Ricki Lake

The first bald patch appeared when Celeste was enrolled in beauty school. A jolt of fear surged through her. *No, it can't happen to me.* Alopecia had robbed Celeste's grandmother of her hair. The patches spread until Celeste's scalp was completely smooth. Initially, she wore wigs. Colorful scarves tied in creative ways to match her outfits and bold earrings provided another covering. She was especially careful around her daughter's teenage friends. Her daughter didn't want Celeste's secret revealed.

One day, her daughter's school called about an emergency. Celeste rushed to the school, forgetting to cover her head. Hurrying through the hallway, young kids gave an accepting nod or "thumbs up." She hurried to finish her business and get home.

After school, her daughter greeted her with a smile. "A lot of people saw you at school today. Know what they said? 'Your mom is so cool.'" Her daughter added, "I'm okay with you being bald."

We may hide our secrets because we know someone cannot handle our truth. Or perhaps we're not ready to face what's happening to us. Sometimes, God keeps certain things secret from us. When the time is right, he reveals his plans in his own way. We cannot fathom all the ways God works, so he asks us to trust him in the hard places.

Hardly any of the Jewish people in Jeremiah's time believed his prophecies. When he warned them they were going to be taken captive, he was ignored, persecuted, and punished. As Jeremiah prophesied, the people were captive for seventy years. However, God wanted them to build homes, plant produce, and marry and multiply (Jeremiah 29:4-6). Despite negative circumstances, God wanted them to thrive!

God's plans for our lives are for good and not disaster, to give us a future and a hope (Jeremiah 29:11). He doesn't forget us in our distress. He wants us to keep living and producing right where we are. We may not see it at first. In time, God will reveal his hand and open it to us with a blessing.

Look in the Mirror

Does it seem like you are just getting by, barely surviving? Does the word "thriving" seem foreign to you? Trust God to be with you during adversity. Continue to press on while you wait for him to bring you through it. He has plans for you.

Prayer

Dear Lord, I want to be rescued from fear and anxiety. Show me how to thrive and conquer during this time. I come to you empty. Fill me with what I need to get through this. Amen.

DESIRING MORE

"There is no chance, no destiny, no fate, that can circumvent or hinder or control the firm resolve of a determined soul."
—Ella Wheeler Wilcox

Only a Little Bit

"Sorry, I can't hear you over the volume of my hair."
—Anonymous

My favorite hairstyle was a texturizer applied on a short cut. By applying a relaxer to my natural hair for a few minutes, I had lots of waves and curls. But my hair straightened over time.

While the relaxer chemical was applied for a few minutes and only to new growth, it had to be shampooed to stop the straightening process. Still, the product continually worked its way along the length of the hair strand until it resulted in a look I didn't want. While it was only a little bit of product on my hair, it ruined the style.

Sin works the same way. It seems like a small amount won't have much effect, but it works into our character and ruins our witness for Christ.

One of the early Corinthian churches turned a blind eye to the situation where a man was living with his father's wife (1 Corinthians 5:1-2). The couple's decision to live together probably started with a few innocent comments.

Maybe the father's son complimented his stepmother. "You're looking beautiful today."

She smiled, her cheeks blushing. "Just today?"

Over time, she might have started complaining about her husband. "I worked hard to prepare your father's favorite meal. Not one 'thank you.'"

"I'm sure he doesn't appreciate you…the way I would." His comment dangled like a lure.

She took the bait. "I could prepare something special just for you."

"Could you bring it to me? Father doesn't have to know."

A little flirting turned into living together, impacting the immediate family and the church's ability to be an effective witness.

The apostle Paul compared the church's tolerance to yeast. "Yeast, too, is a 'small thing' but it works its way through a whole batch of bread dough pretty fast. So, get rid of this 'yeast'" (1 Corinthians 5:6-7, MSG). There is no big or little sin, just as there is no such thing as being a "little pregnant."

Sin takes on a life of its own. In 2 Corinthians 2:8, we find the young man is no longer involved with his father's wife. Paul encouraged the church to forgive and restore him. God does the same with us when we decide to root sin out of our lives. He understands we can't be perfect, but he's ready to forgive, restore, and even help us when we make up our minds to rid ourselves of sinful behavior.

Look in the Mirror

Is there some behavior in your life that you know, or have been told, is sinful but you think is no big deal? When asked to "own it," do you think people should mind their own business? Do you compare it to others who may be doing the same or perhaps worse? Imagine what it would be like to cut that out of your life.

Prayer

Dear Lord, help me not to take sin lightly, but to view it as you do. Help me to be willing to repent so that I can come to you for forgiveness and restoration. Amen.

From the Inside Out

"Does she or doesn't she?
Only her hairdresser knows for sure."
—1956 Clairol® Commercial

P*ssss! Psss!*

"What's that noise?" My sister's voice rose through my cell phone's speaker.

"Color spray. I was doing a quick touch-up on my roots."

"Already? Didn't you just go to the salon to have your roots colored? How often do you have to do all that in-between stuff?"

I was growing defensive. "As often as necessary. What's your point?"

Just over a week after getting my roots touched up, silvery roots glistened around the edges of my face. With my hair parted, gray sparkled in the mirror's lights. I had grabbed a can of root touch-up and sprayed color onto the gray. It was either that or reach for the crayon-like stick to smear color onto the roots. These temporary solutions only coat the hair shaft between shampoos.

My stylist uses permanent hair color. The chemicals open the hair cuticle to remove the natural hair color, and then, using a developer (another chemical), color is deposited back into the strand. This "permanent" color fades after six to eight weeks because it is an external application. Compare that to God transforming us from the *inside* by changing the way we think.

When Jesus preached his message of grace, religious leaders didn't like it. Jesus harshly criticized them. "You blind guides! You strain out a gnat but swallow a camel" (Matthew 23:24). They seemed perfect on the outside, but inside, nothing had changed.

When we accept Jesus, the Holy Spirit renews our mind (Romans 12:2). We think about things that please God. We don't have to adhere to a religious schedule of activities and confessions to make sure we're right with God. He only asks that we allow the Holy Spirit to be the change agent for our renewal.

Look in the Mirror

Consider the things you do "religiously." Some behaviors honor God, such as coming to work on time. Are there any "*rules + faith*" that you think are more acceptable to God? Allow the Holy Spirit to transform you from the inside out.

Prayer

Lord, there are so many false images in the world. What you offer through Jesus Christ has the power to transform. I trust that he is enough and will do the work once and for all. Amen.

Prepare Now

"When I first started wearing wigs, I didn't know you had to anchor them down with bobby pins. I walked out during a windy day and my wig blew off and got stuck to a branch. I was walking while my wig was hanging ..."
—Sherri Shepherd

Ramona chose her wig with care before Sunday morning's church service. She arranged it on her head, finger-combed the bangs across her forehead, and smoothed the back at the nape of her neck. *Maybe I should pin it down.*

"Nah," she said aloud. The wig snuggled tightly against her head. It could last against the Chicago winds. She grabbed her purse and Bible, climbed into her car, and headed out.

She whipped into a parking space in front of the church. "Thank you, Jesus, for prime parking." She stepped out of the car, just as the Windy City lived up to its reputation.

Whoosh! A big gust of wind lifted the wig from Ramona's head. "Lord, Jesus!" The wig tumbled down the street with Ramona running after it. Oh, for the want of a few bobby pins!

Being prepared is important in our daily activities and especially in Christian service as we await Christ's return.

In the parable of the ten virgins, the bridesmaids planned to be part of a wedding celebration. After nightfall, a great procession followed the bridegroom to the bride's house before they returned to his home and continued the festivities. The women fell asleep waiting for the bridegroom. Finally, he came—at midnight. They arose and prepared their lamps to join the procession. Only five had filled them with oil.

The foolish bridesmaids pleaded with the others to give them some oil because their lamps were going out. They were told to go buy some. When they returned, the door to the feast was locked and they weren't allowed inside (Matthew 25:1-12).

The apostle Matthew reminds Christian believers that our bridegroom, Jesus Christ, could return at any time and we must be spiritually ready. He has given us work to do until his return. It could be visiting the sick, writing an encouraging note, or greeting worshippers at the front door. Whatever you do, do it for God's glory (1 Corinthians 10:31).

The lamps of the foolish bridesmaids were useless in the dark. Scripture reminds us that we can prepare for Christ's return by sharing the light of our hope in Christ.

Look in the Mirror

Examine your past "surprises." Would you have prepared more carefully if you'd known what to expect? Is there something you can learn or do differently? Life is filled with uncertainty. Jesus' return is not. Share your light while there's still time.

Prayer

Jesus, I'm looking forward to your return. Help me to faithfully serve others in the waiting. I want to do my part in sharing the hope of a great home-going celebration. Amen.

Is It Worth It?

"My brain cells, skin cells and hair cells continue to die, but my fat cells seem to have an eternal life."
—Anonymous

Jamie shifted uncomfortably under her husband's gaze. Hansen was thousands of miles away, in another country, staring at her Skype® image on his computer.

Hansen leaned close to the screen. "I can see through your hair. What's going on?"

"I'm not sure. The only thing different is the diet I'm following." She told him about the program that would help her lose weight. It cut several food groups and permitted certain others at defined times. "With my schedule, I can only eat twice a day. But I've lost twenty pounds."

Then, something clicked in Jamie's mind. Her hair had started clogging the drain when she shampooed. When raking a hand through her hair, long strands covered her palm. The fine hair framing her face had fallen out.

Jamie's husband rubbed his hair and leaned back in his chair. "Is there anything you can do about your hair?"

"Yes. Give up this crazy diet!" Hair loss was too high a price.

Once she abandoned the extreme diet, her hair grew back. Some things possess immeasurable value and, once lost, can never be regained.

Jesus taught us that our soul is the one thing we never want to risk losing. When Jesus first began talking about the price he'd have to pay for our sins—death on the cross—he also talked about the value of our soul. "What good is it for someone to gain the whole world, yet forfeit their soul?" (Mark 8:36, NIV).

Power. Possessions. Prestige. Even health and beauty are things we can pursue and still wind up with nothing. We will leave these behind since our earthly life is temporary. Instead, Jesus wants us to pursue things with eternal significance, most importantly, a relationship with him.

Look in the Mirror

What do you value? A job? An image? Your standing in the community, church, school, or work? A person? Can you name the price you paid? Time? Relationships? If you were lying on your death bed, would it matter? Choose what will last forever.

Prayer

Father, this world is filled with many tempting things. Help me to recognize the temporary things that I value too highly. I want to shed unimportant things and focus on things with an eternal value like my relationship with you. Amen.

Choosing Present Over Perfect

"The thing that is really hard, and really amazing, is giving up on being perfect and beginning the work of becoming yourself."
—Anna Quindlen

I was going out for the evening and wanted everything to be perfect. Twisting my hair into an updo, one of my locks fell free. The top and bottom were almost as round as a number two pencil, but the middle was whittled to almost nothing. The lock was hanging by a thread, ready to snap.

Was it too much stress from styling, trying to make sure my hair was perfect? Had I neglected proper care, not choosing the right shampoo, conditioner, or oil? I thought I was doing all the right things. I was so self-conscious about my hair that I didn't enjoy my night out. When I visited my stylist, she spelled out my options: let it go right then or hold onto it, although it was bound to break.

Trying to hang onto the illusion of perfection can be stressful. One of Jesus' closest friends had to make a hard choice about perfection or peace.

Jesus and his disciples stopped by Martha's house on their way to Jerusalem. She immediately planned a big dinner. I can imagine her thoughts. *Thirteen guests, including Jesus! The meal must be perfect. What should I serve with the roast lamb? Maybe fish is a better choice. Do I have time to make fresh bread?*

Martha took a deep breath, thankful that she had her sister's help. She looked around the room. "Mary?" Peeking into the living room, she spotted Mary lounging at Jesus' feet. *No way, not today!*

Martha marched into the room and confronted Jesus. "Tell her to help me" (Luke 10:40).

He turned to her and identified the source of her frustration. "You are worried and upset about many things, but few things are needed—or indeed only one. Mary has chosen what is better, and it will not be taken away from her" (Luke 10: 42). He acknowledged Martha had a lot of things going on while also reminding her to choose what was most important.

Most of us have had those Martha-moments where we become overwhelmed trying to achieve perfection and, instead, ended up frayed, frazzled, and frustrated. We can get so caught up that we completely miss the big picture. Is our busy-ness getting in the way? Jesus wants us to be present with him as we quiet our hearts and listen.

Look in the Mirror

Are you feeling "unraveled" by a situation? Is it ongoing or something new? Be honest with God about how you feel. It's not "new news" to him, anyway. Ask him for wisdom to help you see the situation from his perspective. Then give him the problem, let it go, and watch what he does.

Prayer

Jesus, I want to be present with you. I pray that the minor things fade into the background. Let me not be overwhelmed by seeking to be perfect, but to realize that I have perfection when I worship you. Amen.

Making a Clean Break

"People always ask me how long it takes to do my hair. I don't know, I'm never there."
—Dolly Parton

Uma is a youthful-looking woman with platinum hair that twenty-somethings would "dye" to have. When she was nineteen, the first gray strand popped. She was horrified since coal-black hair was the norm in her country. Uma decided on an old-school remedy: hair color. Years later, rashes developed on her smooth caramel skin. She tried antihistamines, and when they didn't work, she sought an acupuncturist.

He met with her after another round of testing. "You've suppressed the symptoms. But you haven't gotten to the root of the problem." He checked her chart, and his gaze shifted to her hair.

Uma shifted uncomfortably at his unbroken stare. *Is my hair out of place? Are my roots showing?*

"Do you color your hair?" he asked. At Uma's nod, he gave a slight smile. "You probably don't want to hear this, but I think you ought to see what happens if you stop."

"But we're moving to America!" she protested.

Uma decided that moving would be a good time to make the change. She wouldn't be recognized in her new country, and the change wouldn't be evident before leaving her birth country. So she made a clean break—from hair color and her old life.

If we could only leave our sinful nature behind like that! The good news is that God won't allow you to be tempted by sinful desires without also providing a way out (1 Corinthians 10:13).

The apostle Paul had a definitive, transformative change from being a persecutor of Christians to a preacher of Christ. Originally known as Saul, he was traveling on his self-assigned mission of pursuing Christians when he was struck blind and Jesus revealed himself. Saul's name was changed to "Paul," and he wrote almost half of the New Testament.

Paul admitted that he wanted to do the right thing, but he often failed (Romans 7:18). If he struggled to make a clean break between his old life and his new one, what hope do we have? The same as Paul: The Holy Spirit who gives us power.

Receiving the Holy Spirit takes a moment of faith. However, fighting the temptation to make wrong choices is a lifelong process, filled with daily battles. We might not start over in another country. But we can begin to make good choices right where we are.

Look in the Mirror

Think of situations that are tempting to you. Maybe it's catching up on the latest gossip. It could be an attraction to someone who's already married or in a relationship. Rehearse a phrase, such as, "I can't join you, today" or "I have other plans." Do you need to take another route to avoid certain people or situations? Ask the Holy Spirit for help in dealing with your struggles to make a clean break.

Prayer

Lord, you know my weaknesses and the areas where I want to break free. Please give me strength and guidance in overcoming this temptation. Amen.

Seekers and Skeptics Welcome

"Just try new things. Don't be afraid.
Step out of your comfort zones and soar."
—Michelle Obama

The salon's number flashed in the window of my cell phone. I casually swiped my finger across the device, anticipating the nature of the call.

Sure enough, the receptionist advised that my stylist no longer worked there. "Would you like to make an appointment with Angela?"

I requested an appointment at the same time and the same day I'd had for the previous year. When I was told that Angela didn't work that day, I sucked in a breath and exhaled. Already, I disliked the changes. My schedule was being disrupted. The new stylist would have to learn my hair. The process of starting over filled me with dread.

I wasn't going to be convinced that Angela and I could work together until she did my hair. Sitting in her chair the next week, Angela lifted my locks and let them fall free. "They're beautiful." Then she stroked the strands of her wig. "I have locks under this. But I just started them. I hope they turn out as good as yours." She studied me in the mirror and smiled. "I'll take good care of them. Want to get started?"

Angela not only knew my hair type and hairstyle, but she was also experiencing it herself. *Poof!* My reservations vanished. It was time to let go of how things had worked with my former stylist and embrace what Angela offered. I nodded, ready to begin anew.

God is the master of new relationships. He invites seekers and skeptics to come to him with doubts. Nicodemus, one of the highest-ranking members of a religious sect, was skeptical about a relationship with Jesus. He approached Jesus at night, acknowledging him as a teacher and miracle-worker. Nicodemus, an old man, didn't understand the talk about being "born again" since he was an old man (John 3:3).

Jesus told him, "For God so loved the world, that he gave his only begotten Son, that whosoever *believeth* in him should not perish, but have everlasting life" (John 3:16, KJV). Jesus experienced what it was like to be human and understands our doubts.

A new beginning is possible through him. "The old life is gone; a new life has begun" (2 Corinthians 5:17, NLT). You don't have to be bound to the past. Believe where you are—questions and doubts included just like Nicodemus. God is ready to lead you on a new, exciting, and life-changing journey.

Look in the Mirror

Perhaps you're experiencing change in some area of your life. Acknowledge what you're feeling. Fear? Doubt? Fatigue? God doesn't resent your questions and wants to reward your search for answers by helping you to find him.

Prayer

Father God, situations and people around me are changing. You remain the same. Help me to keep my eyes where you are leading and not on the past. Amen.

Ignoring Advice

"... I wanted a Chanel bob and bangs. My mom said no. I went to the salon anyway, and they said, 'No way – we are not going to do that to your hair.' So I did it myself. Big mistake. Instead of my bangs going down straight, they were sticking up like a cat. It was horrible."
—Camila Alves

After slogging through heavy traffic on a late Friday afternoon, I arrived at the salon and checked in for my appointment. A flicker of irritation crossed the stylist's face when I reminded her that my appointment included color.

Frowning, she checked her watch. "I guess I have time."

My mind replayed the advice given by a beautician when I received my first relaxer. "Don't let anybody who's in a hurry put a chemical on your hair." Having looked forward to this day for a month, I shoved her words from my mind.

The stylist spoke little as she brushed a warm brown pigment over the black color I had applied at home. An hour later, she stared down at my hair, shaking her head. "It'll be okay if you stay out of the sun."

I could almost hear my former beautician saying, *"Tried to tell you."* A shiver ran through me. *How bad could it be?*

Examining my hair in the mirror, it didn't seem much lighter than when I had arrived. But outside, it was a bright August day. After getting settled in my car, I took a quick peek in the driver's side mirror. *Oh, my!* An inch of brown roots sprouted from the base of my scalp. The dye hadn't taken over the color I had applied at home, so it looked like I had a black mane. Driving home, I kept staring into the mirror. Instead of watching the road, I placed myself and other drivers at risk. If only I'd listened to the earlier warning. Sometimes, we receive wise counsel and ignore it to our detriment.

The Bible story in Acts 27 tells about sailors taking the apostle Paul to Rome. He warned them about dangerous weather conditions. They ignored his counsel, ran into a severe storm, and were shipwrecked for months. Paul reminded them that the loss and damage could have been avoided. He also encouraged them. "Not one of you will lose a single hair from his head" (Acts 27:34, NIV). While I didn't lose hair from the bad dye job, I spent more time and money to correct the problem.

Did you ever experience a feeling of "dis-ease" that you chalked up to nervousness and anxiety? Have you heard a little nagging voice of warning? Did someone trustworthy suggest an alternative? We can't avoid all storms in life, but we lessen the risk of a negative outcome by considering wise counsel.

Look in the Mirror

Are you wrestling with a decision? Do you have reservations? Consider establishing a network of people you trust and respect to help explore alternatives. If you're still conflicted, postpone taking any action until you're at peace.

Prayer

Lord, my heart is set on a certain path. Lead me to wise people to think through my options. Help me be willing to stand still if I have any doubts until I receive clear direction. Amen.

Stripping Down

"If you want to fly, you have to give up the things that weigh you down."
—Toni Morrison

Erin ordered seven ounces of exquisite human hair extensions. They could be worn curly or sleek, blow-dried and flat-ironed, or curled. When the plump bag of hair arrived, she was certain she'd have extra to replace sections or pieces as needed.

She and four friends had arranged for an evening of pampering with an in-demand stylist to do their hair and nails. He arrived for Erin's event two hours late—with an entourage.

Removing Erin's extensions from the bag, he ran his fingers through the hair. "Oh, you'll have lots of movement."

"I'll have some left, right?" Erin asked.

"Don't worry. I know what I'm doing." Although he had brought along a crew, he wouldn't allow anyone to assist him. He did everything, from shampooing to blow-drying, braiding the ladies' hair to anchor the extensions, and cutting and styling. He didn't eat or take a break for four hours. At ten o'clock, he began working on Erin's hair.

She left the party at 3 a.m. and slid into bed with a headache. Her scalp couldn't breathe. Her head felt squeezed as if by a boa constrictor. The stylist had used every strand of hair. Within days, Erin removed several tracks. The hair came out easily as the stitches had gotten increasingly uneven and ragged as he had grown more exhausted. Shaped into an angled bob with layers, the hair had to be cut down to be useful.

The stylist would have done well to consider the warning in the Bible about pride leading to destruction and a haughty spirit to a fall (Proverbs 16:18). His inflated view of himself led to horrible results. Pride is one of the weights that can hinder us in serving others and honoring God.

Paul, in Hebrews 12, describes the Christian life as if it were a race. He tells us to strip off anything that slows us. It doesn't have to be pride. Perhaps it's looking back with regret. Or comparing our progress to another's. Instead of shedding weight, we add bitterness onto the load we're carrying.

We're called to run our own special race—to stay in our lane—and to keep our focus on Jesus. In the Christian race, there is more than one victor. So, let's be faithful to God who called us to this race, knowing that at the end, we'll receive a crown of righteousness.

Look in the Mirror

Can you think of an instance where you became entangled in something other than what you were supposed to focus on? List those things, e.g. anger, regret, jealousy, etc., that trip you. Is there a trigger? Ask God to make you aware of any tendency or situations that provoke you to react with that behavior. Then, when those situations arise, ask God to help you press on with your endeavor.

Prayer

Father, you have called me to a life of service. Help me to lay aside any selfish ambition or anything that would hinder me from serving others. Amen.

Let It Go

"There's not a hair extension or a makeup artist that can make me feel the way I feel when I give back."
—Beverly Johnson

When the volleyball game at the church picnic ended, a petite, dark-haired young woman walked over to the table and sat next to me.

"Lauren!" I exclaimed, recognizing her as the little girl who had immigrated to this country. She was now a college senior. When I had seen her thirteen years earlier, her hair hung past her waist. "What's the story with your haircut? Getting yourself ready for the work world?"

She shook her head. "I donated it to be made into a wig for kids who've lost their hair. I wanted to honor my mom."

When Lauren's mom began losing her hair from cancer treatments, gazing at Lauren's hair gave her pleasure. After her mother's death, Lauren kept her hair long, recalling her mother's joy. One day, Lauren heard a gentle whisper. *"Your hair can bring joy to others."* She shrugged off the thought. Cutting her hair would dishonor Mom. When the whisper became a nagging thought, she began researching an organization that accepted hair donations for children. Lauren prayed about it. Why would giving to someone in need dishonor her mother? Besides, her hair would grow back. She had her hair cut and placed it in the donation envelope, with thanksgiving for blessing her mom and the soon-to-be receiver of her gift.

Sometimes we hold onto things we have no use for—or don't even like—thinking we are respecting a memory or a wish. Maybe it's a hutch filled with crystal that we remove only for dusting. Perhaps it is a gift closet for things we've never given away as intended. Or it could be clothes we bought for ourselves which still have the price tag attached.

Letting go of things that are unnecessary, unneeded, or unwanted can bless someone in need and ourselves, as well. “For God loves a person who gives cheerfully. And God will generously provide all you need. Then you will always have everything you need, and plenty left over to share with others” (2 Corinthians 9:7-8, NLT).

When the Christian church was first established, the new believers worshipped at the Temple daily, met in homes for the Lord’s supper, and shared meals with joy and *generosity*. “They sold whatever they owned and pooled their resources so that each person’s need was met” (Acts 2:45, MSG).

We can always get more stuff. We can honor another’s memory or gift to us by remembering that someone else in need can experience the joy of receiving the item.

Look in the Mirror

What’s in your closet—or storage shed? Are you holding onto things that you don’t like, or intend to use, because they were a gift? Take a picture of the item if you want a tangible memory before letting it go. By releasing it, you will create room in your home and a space for God to fill with a blessing.

Prayer

Lord Jesus, I don’t want my possessions to be the lord of my life. You freely sacrificed yourself for me. I pray to not hold onto things too tightly but to release them to bless others and experience the joy of giving. Amen.

Queen for Life

"I grew up in a world where a woman who looks like me—with my kind of skin and my kind of hair—was never considered to be beautiful. I think it is time that that stops today."
—Zozibini Tunzi, Miss Universe 2019

Diana was crowned as her high school's Homecoming Queen. She looked stunning, as beautiful as a beauty pageant winner. The outgoing queen placed the crown atop Diana's head, adorned by loose, curly, shoulder-length hair, courtesy of a curly perm.

After she graduated, Diana and a friend applied a relaxer over the curly perm. These chemicals should never be mixed. Her hair came out in clumps. It was only weeks away until she was to crown her successor.

Diana and her mom applied gel products to slick Diana's hair down to cover the bald areas—which was most of her head. Despite her hair disaster, she looked regal as she placed a crown atop her successor's head. She didn't allow any issues about hair stop her from appearing before the student body as the outgoing queen following her one-year reign.

Whether it is a high school homecoming, a state, national, or international pageant, there is something about the woman who wears the crown. This woman is a force, a woman with beauty, talents, and smarts.

Our God, the King of Kings, wants women, his queens, to ask him for more. King Solomon, known for his wisdom and wealth, acknowledged the royalty of the Queen of Sheba. This queen was not shabby.

When Sheba determined to find out just how wise Solomon was, she came with more than questions in her mind. "She arrived in Jerusalem with a large group of attendants and a great caravan of camels loaded with spices, large quantities of gold, and precious jewels" (1 Kings 10:2, NLT). She discovered everything she had heard about Solomon's wisdom was true.

She didn't leave with only answered questions. "King Solomon gave the queen of Sheba *whatever she asked for* besides all the customary gifts he had so generously given" (1 Kings 10:13). Sheba had plenty and yet, she asked for more.

God invites us to come boldly before his throne (Heb. 4:16). It's time to stop asking for little things. He considers you as his child, royalty, worthy to wear a crown by virtue of accepting Jesus Christ as your Savior.

What is it you desire? Grace? Mercy? Forgiveness? Love? Dreams? Lift your head knowing that God loves and hears you. "The Lord will hold you in his hand for all to see—a splendid crown in the hand of God" (Isaiah 62:3) When you are God's queen, it's not just for a year. It's for all eternity. Wear your crown well. It looks good on you.

Look in the Mirror

Are you afraid to approach God? Do you think he's more interested in sacrifices or only grants small requests? If earthly kings can grant requests, consider what God is capable of with his resources. He wants you to ask for big things. Go to him in reverence and tell him what you want. Go big.

Prayer

Dear Lord, I come before you with praise and thanksgiving. Thank you for crowning me with glory and righteousness. Now, I seek you for what is in my heart. Amen.

Acknowledgments

Many people helped me to write and shape these devotionals.

To Beth: I'm so grateful we met at the writers' conference. You're a master at writing devotionals, and I'm blessed to learn from you. I love that we've gone from being writing partners to great friends.

To my sister, Audrey: Thanks for listening to my partial edits and changing sentences while reading them to you. Our daily conversations keep us connected, a reminder of the genes we share. Your gentle spirit helps keep me balanced.

To Sharon: From our first meeting, our lives seemed to be mirror images. Being a kindred spirit, you caught the vision for this book and embraced it as if it were your own. You've been my dear friend and tireless encourager.

To my editor, Cathy MacKenzie: For your wisdom and patience.

To my contributors: Thank you for sharing your stories and your input for making them better. I also want to thank the Schaumburg Writers' Meetup Group, who provided feedback, suggestions, and of course, critiques.

Finally, I give honor to God, who wrote the greatest story ever told, of how you relentlessly pursue a relationship with us. Thank you for using me to show how you're involved in things as simple as a single hair. I am amazed you would use me to share your love and provision in all circumstances.

Notes

Called

Sanders-Funnye, S. (2016). Her Voice: A Legacy of Modeling, Mentoring, and OtherMothering. Nova Scotia: MacKenzie Publishing, p. 26

Recognize Tangled Relationships

Hurston, Z. (2006). Their Eyes Were Watching God. New York: Harper Perennial Modern Classics. (Original pub. 1937), p. 55

Revealing Secrets

Lake, R. (2020, January 1). Liberated and Free, Me. Retrieved from https://www/facebook.com/msrickilake/posts/3428553547185648

Quotes

Taken from various sources. One of my favorites was 365 Inspiring Quotes by Inspiring Women 2020 Daily Desktop Calendar, Indiana: TF Publishing.

About the Author

Joanna McGee Bradford is an author, editor, and speaker. She has published nonfiction and fiction, including poetry, devotionals, and articles. Her personal experience stories have been published in magazines such as *Thriving Family* and *Today's Christian Woman*. Her inspirational romance novel *The Father's Voice* was released by Moody Publishers. Joanna has spoken to small groups and at large conferences, including being a guest panelist at the Black Woman's Expo. In addition, she has appeared on radio and television broadcasts. She works as a Risk Manager for one of the world's leading hardlines wholesalers.

Joanna encourages women to take risks in living their best life and finding their ideal career. She has made several career changes, including insurance claims adjuster and manager, police officer, auditor and trainer, and currently, Risk Manager. Joanna enjoys reading (especially memoirs and mysteries), decluttering, painting, and line dancing. She is passionate about helping people to write their stories. She is "Mom" to one son, who serves in the military.

Joanna makes her home in the NW Chicago suburbs.

Visit Joanna at:

www.joannabradford.com

www.ourhairstories.com

Made in United States
North Haven, CT
25 August 2023

40758830R00057